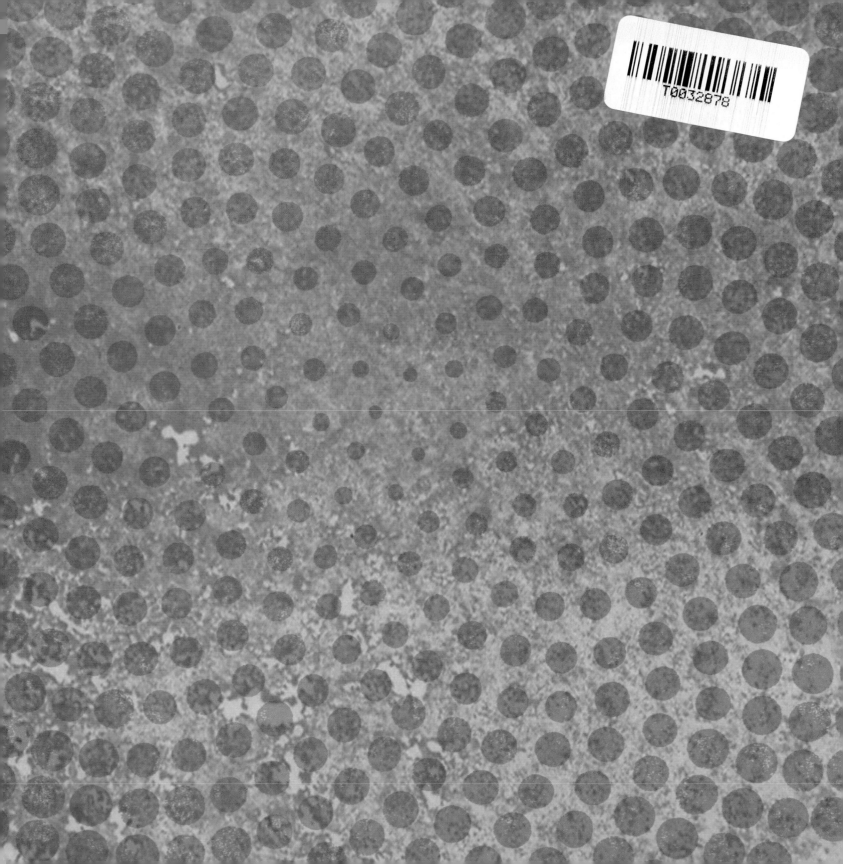

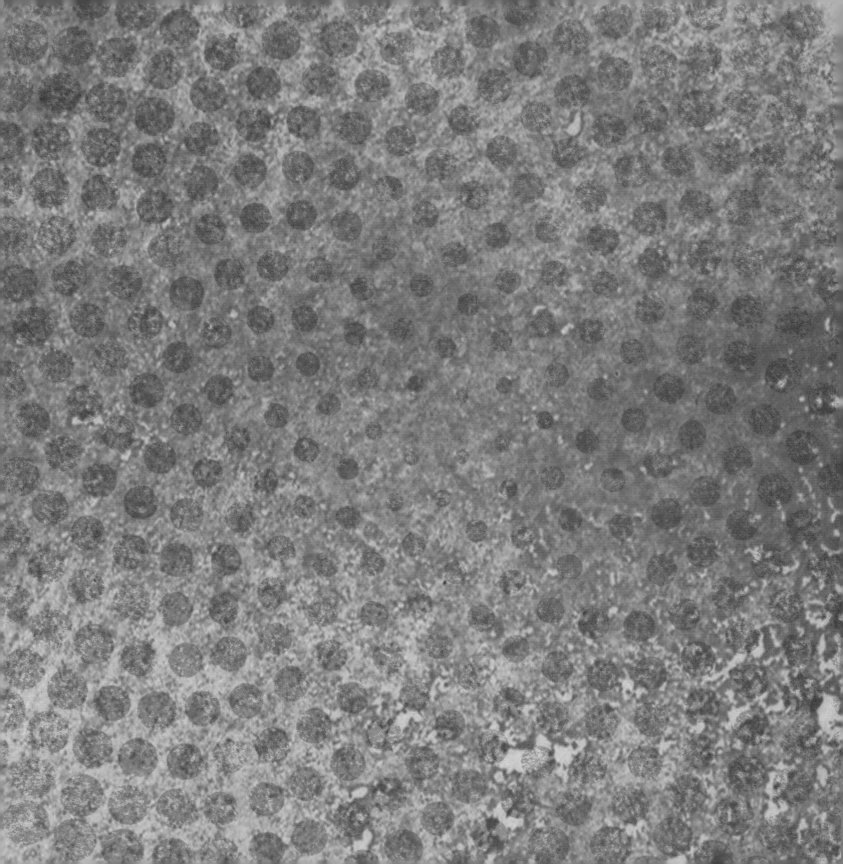

A Seed Grows

Antoinette Portis

NEAL PORTER BOOKS

HOLIDAY HOUSE / NEW YORK

A

seed

falls

and settles into the

soil

and the

shines

and the

rain

comes down

and the seed

and

into the open air

and the plant

grows

and

and

grows

until it forms a

bud

that blossoms into a

flower

which fills with

that drop to the ground
and feed the

birds

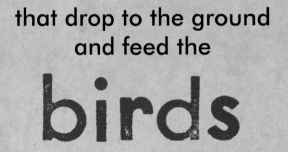

that nest in the leaves

in the tops of trees

where the sun shines.

And a

seed

falls.

Parts of a sunflower seed

Striped shell
This hard shell protects the seed inside until the conditions are right for sprouting or germination.

Seed
The seed itself is made up of a tiny baby plant and food for that plant to fuel its germination.

What the seed needs to sprout

Soil

Soil offers a safe place for a seed to sprout, as well as providing needed minerals.

Sun

A sunflower seed starts to grow when the sun warms the soil.

Water

Water needs to enter a seed to start its growth.

Air

A seed also needs oxygen to germinate.

Parts of a sunflower plant

The flower is an important part of the plant. The large, petaled structure actually contains hundreds of tiny flowers in the center! When pollinated, each little flower produces a new seed.

The bright color of flower petals attract pollinators like bees and butterflies.

Leaves gather energy from sunlight and turn it into food for the plant through a process called photosynthesis.

The stem, or stalk, holds the leaves up to sunlight. Inside, it has channels that carry water and food around the plant.

Roots not only anchor the plant, they draw water and minerals up from the soil to help the plant grow.

Seed sprouts

Stem, leaves, and roots grow

Seeds disperse

Life Cycle of a Sunflower Plant

Bud forms

Seeds form

Flower blooms

More to explore

Chace, Teri Dunn and Llewellyn, Robert. *Seeing Seeds*. Timber Press, 2015.

Farndon, John. Seeds. *World of Plants*. Blackbirch Press, 2006.

Gibbons, Gail. *From Seed to Plant*. Holiday House, 1991.

Page, Robin. *Seeds Move!* Beach Lane Books, 2019.

Rattini, Kristin. *Seed to Plant*. National Geographic Readers. National Geographic
 Partners, 2014.

Richards, Jean. *A Fruit is a Suitcase for Seeds*. The Millbrook Press, 2002.

Robbins, Ken. *Seeds*. Atheneum Books, 2005.

Stone, Lynn. *Seeds*. Rourke Publishing, 2008.

How to grow sunflowers from seeds: https://www.wikihow.com/Grow-Sunflowers

For Sasha and Maziyar, who helped me come back to life.

The author wishes to thank
The Children's Education staff at Brooklyn Botanic Garden

Neal Porter Books

Text and illustrations copyright © 2022 by Antoinette Portis
All Rights Reserved
HOLIDAY HOUSE is registered in the U.S. Patent and Trademark Office.
Printed and bound in March 2023 at Toppan Leefung, DongGuan, China.
The artwork for this book was created using various printmaking
techniques, including gel printing, linocutting, potato stamping
and printing with a celery stalk.
www.holidayhouse.com
First Edition

10 9 8 7 6 5 4 3

Library of Congress Cataloging-in-Publication Data

Names: Portis, Antoinette, author.
Title: A seed grows / by Antoinette Portis.
Description: First edition. | New York : Holiday House, [2022] | Series: A
 Neal Porter book | Includes bibliographical references. | Audience: Ages
 4 to 8 | Audience: Grades K–1 | Summary: "An educational picture book
 about the life cycle of a sunflower"— Provided by publisher.
Identifiers: LCCN 2021037881 | ISBN 9780823448920 (hardcover)
Subjects: LCSH: Seeds—Growth—Juvenile literature.
Classification: LCC QK731 .P599 2022 | DDC 575.6/8—dc23
LC record available at https://lccn.loc.gov/2021037881

ISBN: 978-0-8234-4892-0 (hardcover)